Beautiful Symmetry: The Story of Emmy Noether

Copyright © 2017 Jessica Christianson. All rights reserved.

No part of this book shall be reproduced or transmitted in any form or by any means.

Published by Girls Rock Math

For more copies of this book, please email: jessica@girlsrockmathematics.com

Written by Jessica Christianson

Illustrated by Brittany Goris

Although every precaution has been taken in the preparation of this book, the publisher and author assume no responsibility for errors or omissions. Neither is any liability assumed for damages resulting from the use of information contained herein.

WHEN EMMY NOETHER WAS A GIRL, THERE WAS A

Bicycle craze!

Bikes were the newest invention, and everyone was riding them. People loved to ride, and Emmy was no exception. She would travel all over the streets of Erlangen, her little home town in Germany. She was fearless on two wheels. She would zip down alleys, and fly down hills. She would whip past her brother Fritz.

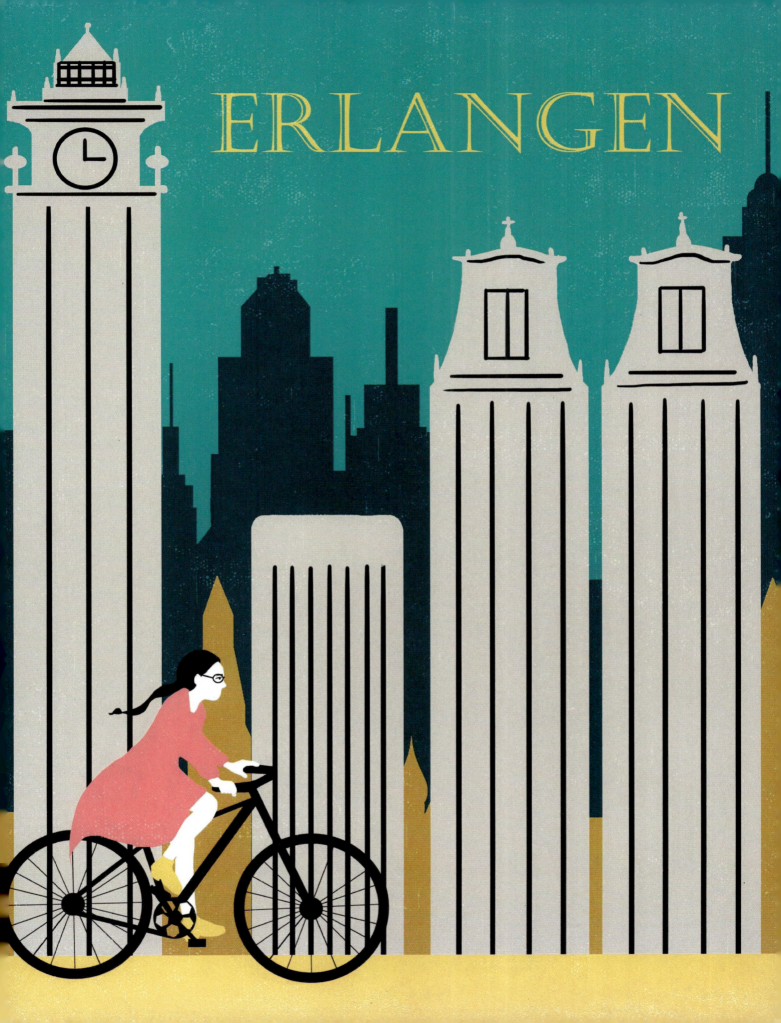

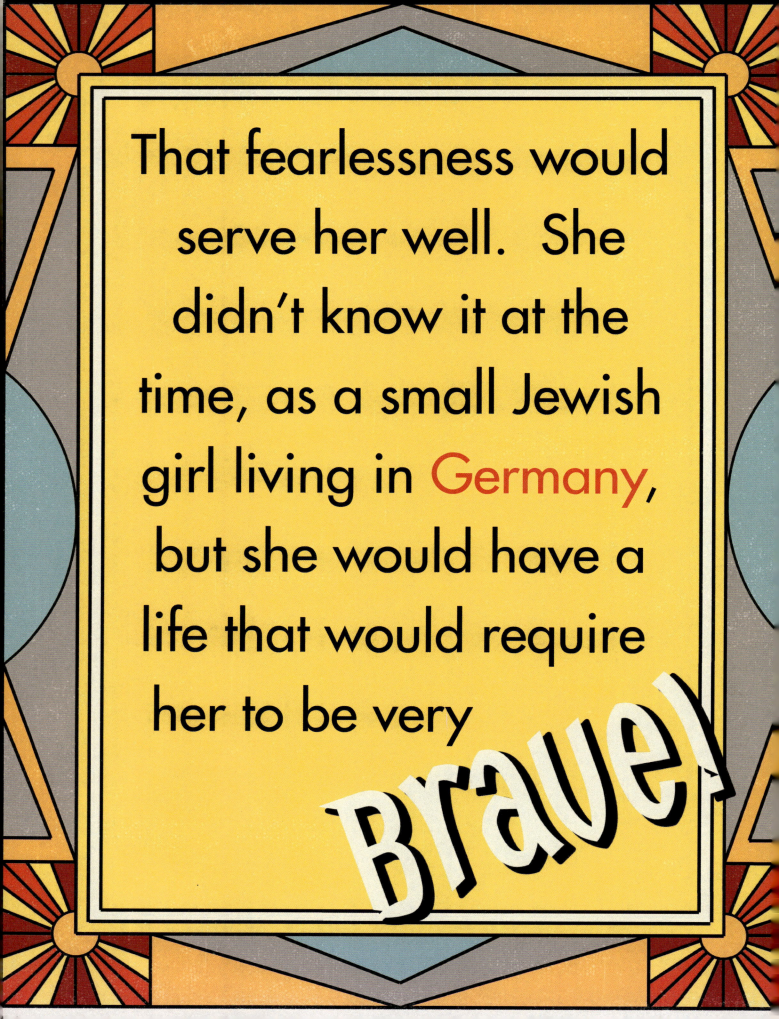

That fearlessness would serve her well. She didn't know it at the time, as a small Jewish girl living in Germany, but she would have a life that would require her to be very Brave!

WHEN EMMY WAS BORN her mother and father adored her, like any parent would adore a child. THEY CALLED HER **Amalie** or **EMMY** for short. She was a bright and curious baby, always smiling up at them from her crib.

Emmy's father, a brilliant mathematician at the university, wanted his children to love math as much as he did. He would turn any common situation into a chance to introduce them to numbers.

He would ask Emmy questions like:

"You have three dolls, if Mama and I gave you three more, how many would you have?"

EMMY wouldn't reply. She just smiled at him.

3 + 3

When she was ten and riding her bicycle all around town, her father would say, "If you ride 6 miles every day, how many miles will you ride after a week?" She would go back to pumping her tires, smiling to herself.

Her father said to her mother, "I guess girls really aren't much for math. Good thing Fritz is following in my footsteps." Emmy's brother Fritz enjoyed math. Like his father, he studied math at the university and became a mathematician. Girls in Emmy's time rarely went to college. They often taught things like English or Piano.

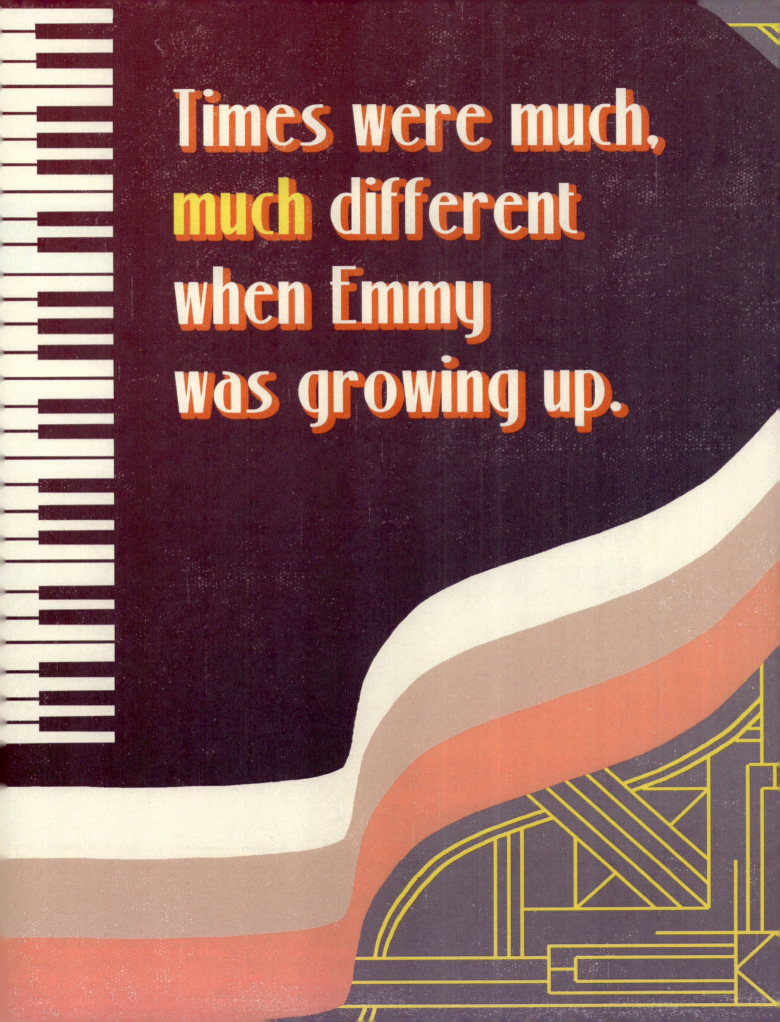

But Emmy was not an **ORDINARY** girl!

EVEN THOUGH IT WAS UNCOMMON FOR GIRLS TO GO TO COLLEGE...

SHE DECIDED TO DO SOMETHING **BRAVE!**

Just like her father and brother She decided to go to school to study **MATH**

That didn't stop her; she sat in on the classes anyway. In those days in Germany, a college degree was given if a man could pass a final test at the end of all his years of school. When Emmy took the test not only did she pass, she did better than any of the actual students! The University noticed her high scores and allowed her into the graduate school as the first woman to ever attend.

She finished her PhD, and became a Doctor of Mathematics.

After that, Emmy still had to find a job. No one at the University would give her one. They were afraid of what people would say about a female professor, so she worked for free as an assistant to the male teachers. When she wrote books, she used a man's name. She was brilliant, but no one would allow her to be herself. She had to be very patient.

Emmy worked for free for the first 7 years of her career. Finally one of the University officials said, "This is not a locker room! What does it matter if she is a woman?" They listened to him and hired her, but for much less pay than the male professors. To prove she was their equal, Emmy decided to go swimming in the men's pool every morning just because she could.

Have you ever forgotten to put the kickstand down on your bike? What happens? It falls over, of course! Why doesn't it tip over when you're riding it? Emmy's work in math proved why a bicycle is safe to ride. Gravity, motion, and speed keep the wheels turning. The math Emmy did was able to prove why these elements work together so well. It's because there is symmetry hidden inside nature's laws!

Where do you see symmetry in a bicycle?

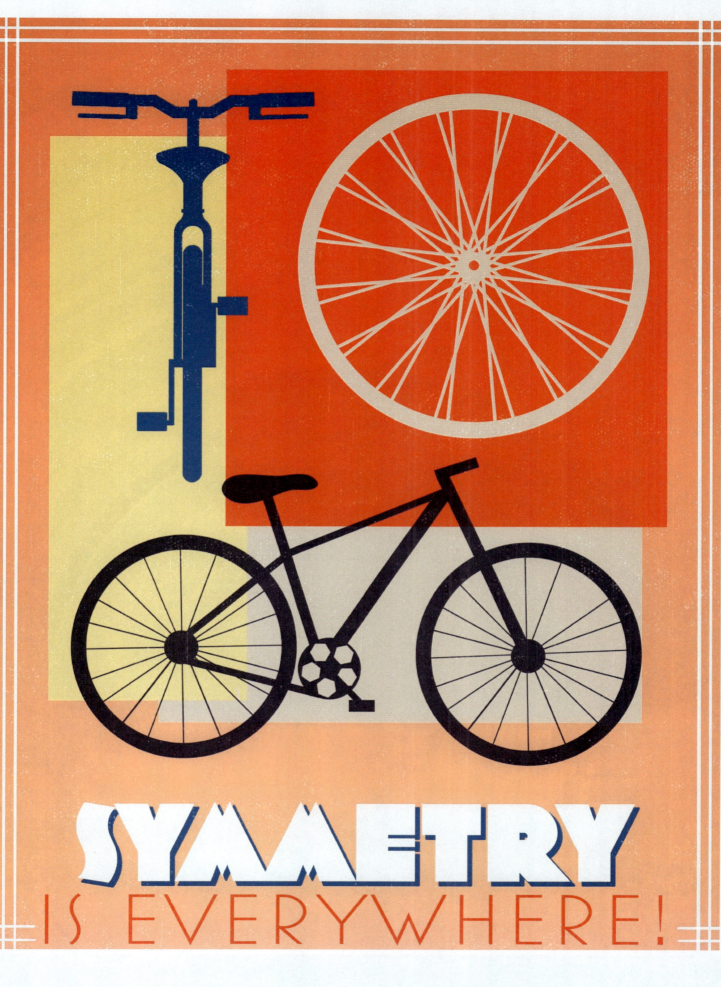

IT WAS A GOOD THING
EMMY WAS SO BRAVE

Terrible things were happening in Germany in the 1930s.

THERE WAS AN AWFUL
WAR GOING ON

EMMY WAS NOT SAFE!

Emmy found herself working in America. She worked alongside Albert Einstein, and became the head of the Math Department at Bryn-Mawr College. People called Emmy amazing, striking, and inspirational. Albert Einstein said she was a creative genius! That was a lot coming from a genius like Einstein. More than anything else, that really made her smile!

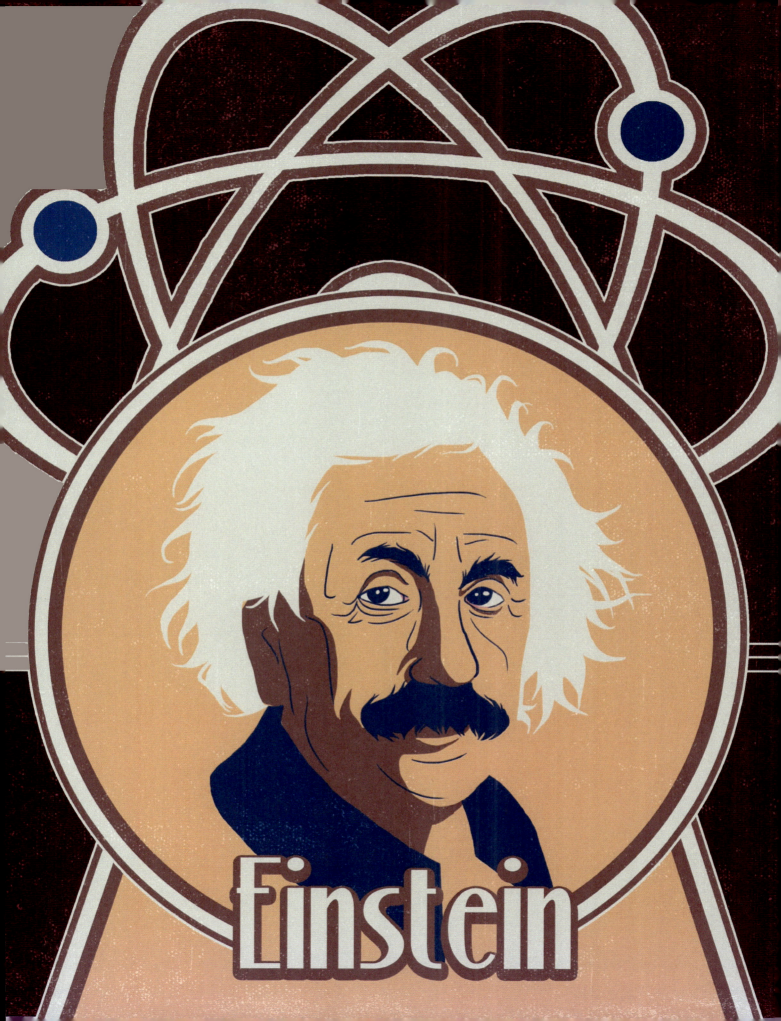

Timeline of Emmy Noether's Life

1882
Emmy is born in Erlangen on March 23

1900
Emmy teaches at a girls school and audits math classes

1903
Emmy passes the math exam for the University

1907
Emmy recieves her doctorate degree in Mathematics

1915
Emmy is offered a paid job at the Univtersity

1933
Emmy escapes Germany and takes a position at Bryn-Mawr

1935
Emmy Noether dies

STORY DISCUSSION

WHAT DO YOU THINK?

1. When Emmy was young she wasn't interested in math at all. What do you think changed?

2. When Emmy was a writer she had to use a man's name. Do you think women still do that today? Why or why not?

ABOUT THE AUTHOR
JESSICA CHRISTIANSON

Jessica is a former elementary school teacher who created the Girls Rock Math program to empower more girls to be confident in math. Writing these books about inspiring women in the field of mathematics is one way she hopes to inspire girls

Afterword

Emmy's Work

Emmy Noether worked in a field of mathematics called abstract algebra. One of the things that this kind of mathematics looks at, is taking away any information that isn't necessary for solving a problem. Then, a problem that may seem very challenging at first may end up being much simpler with the extra information gone.

Read the problem below and decide what information is extra and not needed in order to solve the problem.

Emmy and her brother Fritz rode their bikes into town. It was a 12 minute bike ride from their home to the library. They stayed at the library for 20 minutes, each checked out 4 books, and then rode their bikes straight home. How long were Emmy and Fritz gone?

What information did you take out?

Answer: The number of books they checked out.

Another way to explore abstract algebra is with fun problems like this…

when does 2 + 5 = 1?

When you change the way you think about numbers, that's when! Emmy spent a lot of time thinking about groups of numbers. Imagine you have a set of numbers 0, 1, 2, 3, 4, 5. This is the entire set— just these six numbers. If you arranged them in a circle like on a clock, and to add you went around the clock in a clockwise motion, you would only ever go from 0 to 5 and back again. No matter what, you could only land on 0, 1, 2, 3, 4, or 5.

Using this clock face, if you started on zero and added 2, you would land on 2. But if you were already on 2 and added 5, instead of getting 2 + 5 = 7, you'd have 2 + 5 = 1!

Try these problems:

3 + 4 =   4 + 2 =   5 + 4

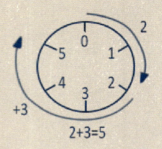
2+3=5

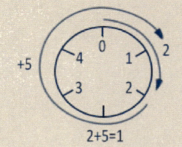
2+5=1

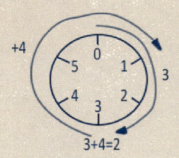
3+4=2

Are there any problems you can create that are the same on the clock face as they are on a number line?

Bonus: What would happen if you used a clock that went up to 12?

Answers:

0 + 1, 0 + 2, 0 + 3, 0 + 4, 0 + 5

1 + 1, 1 + 2, 1 + 3, 1 + 4

2 + 2, 2 + 3

There are all kinds of ways to think about numbers, and Emmy was someone who enjoyed thinking about math in new and interesting ways. When you open your mind up to new possibilities, you can find there are all kinds of ideas out there!